*I'd ask you to join me by the
Río Bravo and weep...*

Jorge Humberto Chávez

*I'd ask you to join me by
the Río Bravo and weep
but you should know
neither river nor tears
remain*

translated from Spanish
by Lawrence Schimel

Shearsman Books
with Vaso Roto Ediciones

First published in the United Kingdom in 2017 by
Shearsman Books
50 Westons Hill Drive
Emersons Green
BRISTOL
BS16 7DF

Shearsman Books Ltd Registered Office
30–31 St. James Place, Mangotsfield, Bristol BS16 9JB
(this address not for correspondence)

www.shearsman.com

ISBN 978-1-84861-515-1

ACKNOWLEDGEMENTS
This volume was originally published in Spanish by the
Fondo de Cultura Económica, Mexico City, Instituto Cultural de Aguascalientes,
Aguascalientes, Ags., Mexico, Instituto Nacional de Ballas Artes, Mexico City and
Conaculta (Consejo Nacional para la Cultura y las Artes, Mexico City.

This translation is published by arrangement with
Vaso Roto Ediciones, Monterrey & Madrid.

Credits in order of appearance:

Jorge H.: Journalist. Dallas, TX.
Natalia: Nutritionist. Juarez City.
Deimy: College Student in El Paso, TX.
Rosy: Student and housewife in San Luis Potosí.

1.

CHRONICLES

Satan

105 pins have stopped the flow of your naked petals five-year old
butterfly of the Bravo del Norte river

like a ship in the middle of the light advancing the afternoon toward
the flank of the western hills you would play there on the sidewalk

while your mother and the neighbor from across the street made much
to do of the inanities that fill our lives

the sun sets the cars roll across the unpaved street and the crepuscular
air bears the whisperings of the evil God like chords

to the ears of the woman who sees you playing every day in front of
her house and your mother gets up and says I'll be back

and will never see you again

the woman approaches and takes your hand and with you crosses the
dust raised by the automobiles

you reach the miserable dwelling where the voice of God insists
stick a pin in her and another

and another pin until reaching 105 of them in order to halt that voice
and the sun winds up entering beneath the hills

and the dust from the cars settles over the world

Chronicle of My Ghosts

my father had the wise idea of taking refuge in a hospital

and dying on the same day

that the people voted for the new government

and he never managed to see

how they began falling like flies

first those from the other side of the city

then those from the adjacent colonia   later acquaintances

then the neighbors

and finally the sunset gave us the death of a friend

and of a brother

and the city like a hunted animal and the motorists who move
quickly quickly watching from the corners of their eyes the driver
next to them who watches in the rear view mirror the driver behind

while the police the judge and the thief come to an agreement saying now it's your turn and then yours and the beast began to lose the sheen of its coat and later its skin

just look at you now you've become a small animal

with its eyes in the sockets of its children

wandering blind and heartless through the cities

The Man in White Shorts
Makes Me Think of My Father

For Miguel Ángel Chávez Díaz de León

María de la Luz used to knit the morning sun and turn it into a big
tray of *pan dulce* in the center of the table of my boyhood with my
siblings

Saturday was for washing grandfather's truck a blue '55 Chevrolet
Saturday itching to flee from God on Sunday morning

the young recruits from Fort Bliss with their long sedans saying good-
bye to their girls as if they were going for a stroll into the line of fire

the border like a splendid animal sprawled out on the grass cultivated
with its flank shining with reflected light

I remember cleaning the windshield and seeing him peer around the
far corner carrying a small box in his hands

I remember saying in a high voice Mamá someone's coming I think
that man's my father and it sure was

he had been arrested the day before in Denver while having lunch at
the mattress factory on Stuart Street

and he begged to retrieve the box from his locker because in it were
our Christmas cards and some photos

I remember this like some Paradisiacal etching because war and
deportation were something else of course

now driving down the avenue I pump the brakes because that man in white shorts

is just sprawled there with a gunshot that has gouged out a small bloodless hole in his left cheek

while I'm on my way to see you

Another Chronicle

On October 6th of the year of his death, Armando El Choco told us
at a party that they had come looking for him

and they found him a month later one morning while he was warming
up the motor of his car before taking his daughters to school

in 1967 we went to the Río Bravo to wash the neighborhood cars first
Chato's then Bogar's and finally Huarache Veloz's

in 1990 the police went to the Río Bravo to pick up the young girls
who waited on the shore to cross over to El Paso

in the year 2010 the river now almost parched an immigration officer
and 13-year-old Sergio Adrián fought the boy with a stone in his hand
and the agent with a revolver

that same year at a corner store in the Salvácar neighborhood the clerk
refused to hand over protection money and received a bullet in the
face

and 17 of his neighbors were hunted down one by one as they
celebrated winning a game of touch football

oh young son of Cadmus I know you'd rather be elsewhere but today
you are here sang old Ovid

and you a woman they dragged from home and threatened to kill your
husband if you didn't get in for your last car ride

I'd ask you to join me by the Rio Bravo and weep but you should know there's no longer any river there and nor are there tears

Seven Postcards from the End of the World

1. The word *pickup* on a hill is like an altar with its purple backdrop of clouds wounded by the evening sun

2. Fear is the name of the avenue that stretches full of lights and without any cars one Saturday at ten p.m. on the northern border

3. That young girl on the verge of a roundabout who stops drivers and tells them take me wherever you wish for 200 pesos has no first or last name

4. Dirt yard with a pile of large round rocks in the background and a woman beneath the moon braiding the ghost girl's hair

5. Rayón street neighbors playing *lotería* by the light of the lamppost singing the names of El Diablo and La Muerte announcing the years when they'll come

6. A couple arguing about the chairs and lamps in their house while on the sidewalk out front their neighbor is dying with four shots to the chest

7. Delia admiring her naked body in the wardrobe mirror without realizing that a visiting 6-year-old boy is on the sofa

7.1. And he takes note of her splendorous beauty to put it before your eyes

7.2. 40 years later

Birthday

The world is simple when you're nine years old the rain for example
always comes from the west washing the pebbles from the street

there is no east: just north and west the word sun is from the west
the word river remains in the north the word wet is north as well

war meant Fort Bliss or Vietnam and the word papá meant
Denver or an old Chevrolet waiting for its owner

papá is north the word country was difficult it was neither west nor
north country it seemed to imply city though most used it more as
neighborhood

in the shelter of the Franklin mountain which was north and the
western sunsets and desert storms the word south appeared

that same day came the word massacre: it meant three hundred
students suddenly shot in a plaza

country was not then the house it was instead a strange border where
things happened that you didn't dare speak of

mother is like a large tray of *pan dulce* and the word country instead
means not having any bread at all on the table

it is not difficult then to understand what they mean at age nine
by the word massacre the word south the word country

That Morning I Had Quit Smoking
(09-11-01)

Of all the vices I have the cigarette is the one that gives me the least
pleasure I'd told you early that morning

foundering in the maelstrom of a hangover bringing my head to the
jet of cold water fighting against the tang of smoke in my mouth

the television mumbled the news in a strange rhythm
urgent voices quick turns bunched up words

you went back to sleep and an image appeared on the screen of a
tower
burning and another Babel of reports and notes

it was the North: *coño y carajo*: I managed to hear myself and I said
wake up something is happening in New York this can't be

you stirred a little and continued dreaming of the Cielo Vista Mall
putting all its brand-name clothes out in the aisles

when the second plane appeared flying very low and unhurriedly so
that the cameras could follow it clearly

and catch it crashing against the South Tower and the fire and I think
I managed to see a desk ejected amid office paperwork

I glanced at the nightstand for my cigarettes but I remembered that I
had decided to give up smoking and I returned to the television

you need to wake up like *now* the world is changing before us right
there on the television screen

there is no hangover that can handle the fact that God signed his
resignation letter that morning in the neighbor's house

there is no simile or metaphor for this: the 85th floor of the South
Tower fell upon the 84th floor and then both upon

the 83rd floor and then all three upon the 82nd and so on for close to
10 seconds until reaching the basement itself

and then the North Tower followed and I only managed to hear you
say very softly *Jee-zus* and me I can't even wake up

later in my car heading to the office everything was normal except for
a cement barricade that blocked access to Lincoln Avenue

the American consulate closed the international bridge closed the
Abraham González airport closed

and then the snake-like rows of cars crossing the border at a standstill
for hours with their colors under the sun

gas prices rising plane tickets skyrocketing the cost of Louis Vuitton
bags rising cigarettes at double their original price

2006

In 2006 my father lost so much weight
we were able to fit his body into a box
measuring 1.70 by .65m

I myself began to lose humanity
with the demon deep inside
86 kilos in February 69 in July

In 2006 love lost so much weight
that a mere breeze could knock it across
to the other side of the border line

In the year 2006 my country began to lose weight
the street and the night increasingly thinner
the city flooded with cadavers

Chronicle of the Belltower

The meridian has just passed between the scant trees of this street
about to enter its dark stratum

car engines resound on this corner of the El Campa neighborhood
a dog stops before crossing to the other sidewalk

four young men are standing with their backs against the wall surround-
ing the Pedro Medina school still thinking that nothing will happen

their steps had taken them far from home that morning to make their
ways to the meeting at 12:40

and it is here that the music begins on Paseo de los Compositores
someone shouts the dog flees silently down the street

body A falls immediately clear brown skin twenty years old regular
complexion dressed in blue

some bullets pierce the mortar blocks of the wall and fall into the patio
where the children are playing basketball

body B falls slightly upon A white shirt 5'6" wearing jeans and dying
at the age of twenty three

the kids drop their ball and run toward the classrooms where their
professors shoot the breeze and sip sodas

body C twenty years old is thin and brown but his shirt is purple and
he's still wearing a black cap

a young woman who heard the shots in front of her door emerges
soulless to search for her daughter at the corner store

the fourth youth manages to run but falls bathed in bullets and sunlight
in the center of the street and his face is left in a pothole in the asphalt

there the young woman finds him and notes that his breathing raises
a fine cloud of earth that rises with the air from his nostrils

he is 5'3" is also dark wears a gray shirt and sneakers lived only twenty
years: body D

the paths of life are not what I expected is being sung to us now by a
melancholy vallenato

from a distant stereo amid the narrow houses that have had to close
their windows and doors

a bus drives by deafening the light of midday and breaking the order
that death has installed on this street

the trees watching from the sidewalk remain still but on this November
day they will refuse to cast their shade

The River

The city is one. One dirty river splits it in 2: swamp of sweat.
Poetry is many: words which transmute as soon as you cross this river.
A glance scrutinizes from the bushes the green path though the water.
Here is the end of the closed heart, the end of an orphan country;
other meanings begin here.

The red river separates the city and in every universe it assembles its history
of party or nightmare Barely across the boundary that same voice prays
other realities. From this shore there is blood upon the rocks
and on the other the weapon still seeks its target: skin bathed in lean
moons against the sibilance of metal. But the city remains one.

There is a dark river advancing through the city, a river armed
at night between the shafts of the buildings. It divides the city into black
and white. The south is a shout; the north is a party of light. This river
advances beneath the bridges like a machete reaping cotton.
The city aches and sings, but beneath the light of the sun it remains just one.

The Escobar Avenue Morgue

How to know who came to this house how if the doors have not
closed for as long as I can remember

and those who entered from the north should vacate quickly quickly
through the exit that leads to the west

with barely enough time to lie on their backs a moment to wait
for someone to come and to say

this young woman is named Rocío this man is Julián although they
can no longer answer from their being so asleep

listening to the steps that come from the sidewalk amid the noise of
the cars and the tumult of dissolution itself

in an attempt to recognize the rhythm of a footstep and thus to notice
how true it is to not know how to return to the vigil

this is what there is: a breeze that carries a scent of defeated days and
bodies that seem to be at rest

a knee slightly upraised a hand with its palm visible
some lips that try to smile and don't know how

and that blonde young woman with bare breasts who has her mouth
at your ear and who tells you the dreams she lost in eternity

Austin Triptych
Dec. 31

I. Searching for the Little Longhorn Bar

The public program Photographs for Common Citizens of Austin
allows for the recording of the faces of those people that no one sets
their eyes on

and there are men and women that no one sees but what's worse is
that they know it and this happens because

cities live hurriedly and we who live in them move
at such a rhythm that despite our affiliation to the city and
the equal importance of everyone

we wind up not seeing the others perhaps in the same way in which
sometimes we walk down entire streets thinking of empty hotels

and we imagine that no one in their home is awake that the few
who move down the streets are each sinking into their own hole that
there are no longer any people

and that this is due to no one seeing us

2. Martha Harding, Waitress

From table to table

between happy chords and songs Martha serves white wine and beer
in the Little Longhorn Bar on Barnett St.

she says she's served drinks in the bars of Austin for as long as she can
remember and I think that perhaps she did so in 1979 when I dreamed

with all my very young might to travel from Juarez and come
to the university to crash the class of Professor J.L. Borges

it would be an exaggeration to say that Martha Harding once served a
drink to Mr. Borges but I am sure she did to many of his disciples

as she serves one to me and that is all that I have in common with the
beloved Argentine master

it is true that it took me thirty years to come to Austin with Borges but
my consolation is that I arrived at last

how poor is the consolation of the heart when the ifs are
its only remedy

3. May You Have a Prosperous New Year

A bottle of wine and a table on which to place the bottle and a house
in which to set down the table

bread and fruit are the nourishment of angels and a bit of roast for
your simple human part

here in the New Year's party in Austin we are joined by Leonel
and his girlfriend Samia who has come from Egypt

from Ciudad Juárez came Deimy Yolanda with Natalia and Jorge H.
Chávez Ramírez

for all of them peace in their tormented souls and for their countries
a new heart

happy mouths and eyes because the dark ones having seen and spoken
are living closer to death

another God for all less a friend of luxury and usury closer to those
who search for him to be more human and simpler

the infallible hand of a love which on resting on your head gives you
heat and calm on those thick blue nights

without a single star nor refuge nor hope

The Collapse

Beneath the flesh you find the smooth lumber of the bones

before the bullet

which is definitive and has precise teeth with the flame in the journey
that ignites its whistling all skin is fragile

a straight smooth edge a minimal slow crackling fingers that are
almost caresses

opening you muscle and sense

skin is so fragile the flow of blood so vulnerable

on this long day of sun from this charred city I speak to you of grief
and of the wound

2.

Snapshots

Father Balthazar

Now, every time I approach mirrors I see you more while slowly, very
slowly, my own face is erased, father

birds flutter above us with their conical beat because life has complicated
everything for us women children love poetry

I know that some morning your countenance and mine will wind up the
same in the bed of some hospital the color of our eyes washed out

but today the country has still dawned wrapped in the scent of coffee
and in bed there's a lovely young woman who dreams of the future

everything immersed in an uncommon beauty

Chronicle of Père Lachaise
or The Walk of the Dead

Hey mister maestro Guillaume Apollinaire now that I think of it we also
won a war on the north front

against their hard hearts against the dark power of money
against usury of the spirit

that's why I went to look for you that afternoon in Paris and that's why
before reaching the cemetery I bought a bit of wine and a bottle opener
at a kiosk

on entering I suddenly heard a voice among the tombs the unmistakable
voice of Juanjo Rodríguez who should be in Mazatlán

he was acting as the guide for a group of Spanish tourists, that Juanjo,
posing as a guide for some Spanish girls

after the surprise and greeting one another I joined the group and Juanjo
led me to the tomb of Jim the Lizard King and I told him

that this was fine but that I needed to find your tombstone because I'd
promised you some wine thirty years before

oh old professor I saw so many things with your eyes I loved so much
with your words and now walking among the *flock of the bridges*

with wine in the pockets of my gabardine wine just for you a wine like
a shining coin

Marcial another man of letters from Mexico was also there
and we left the young ladies to go and meet you old Apollinaire

two hours reading on tombs names as vulgar as those of
Auguste Comte Isadora Duncan and Colette

and suddenly among those marble slabs was GUILLAUME
APOLLINAIRE DE KOSTROWITZKY 25 AOÛT 1880. 9 9ᴮᴿᴱ
1918 — JACQUELINE APOLLINAIRE 1891-1967

the sun stung toward the fields in the distance and I had never been
so close to greatness as on that afternoon beside you

I opened the bottle of wine barely sniffed it and poured the first stream
where your head should be and I said

my name is Jorge and I think that I owe you some loves and I owe you
poetry and I come from Mexico to drink a toast with you

with you I toast your feet and I poured wine with you I toast your right
hand and I poured wine and with you I toast your left hand

and I toast Jacqueline the Beautiful Redhead and I pour away the rest
of the alcohol onto the tomb and Marcial shouted Jorge leave a little

no sir I told him this bottle is for Guillaume Apollinaire but don't
worry because there are two pockets in my gabardine

and I uncorked the second bottle and we began to drink straight from
the bottle and the world approached its culmination

on the way back I refused to offer wine to Alfred de Musset to Sara
Bernhardt and to a poseur named Allan Kardec

not so with Frédéric Chopin to whom I poured a tipple *O Eiffel Tower*
shepherdess this morning the bridges are bleating

have pity on us who always fight on the borders of the unlimited and what
is to come

That Man Seated on the Bench
Is Named W.C. Williams

Once
   at El Paso,
      toward evening,
  I saw – and heard! –
   ten thousand sparrows
       W.C.W.

Interstate 10 is long and from it you can see the light of
Júarez below El Paso Texas above

great warehouses of glass on their sides and 2 and a half million
people dreaming in different languages

dreams of land and of metal dreams of children on their bicycles
wandering between the factories dreams of trains as bridges

in 1911 from El Paso one could see Villa's men
firing their rifles from west to east

to avoid a stray bullet hurting the tourists who watched
our revolution from their comfortable terraces

and twenty years later we went to the Paso del Sur and so much whiskey
ran through the streets that the drunken binge lasted 59 years

women and men without any hope found their fatherland
and their truth in the voice and the pelvis of Elvis the King

near the Mississippi a black lady named Rosa Parks took
her daily bus ride and changed the face of America forever

at the start of the 70s a bullet left a book warehouse
and ricocheted off a dark Lincoln and came to rest in the walls
of a theater

then we could see American youths in their war leaving behind their
cars and their girlfriends

others crossed over the rungs of the air and disembarked on the moon
with their huge white boots

but now that I'm being served a second drink in this bar on Mesa Street
I think none of this was important

unless it was that night when you saw and heard ten thousand sparrows
come from the desert to this same plaza

and you said the words that have made you great:

this was I,
        William Carlos Williams,
                            I did my best;
farewell.

Mother

There is a window on Fierro street
in the house at number 300 there is a window
there is an April night in that house's window
a date that is still in the window of Fierro 300
if you look closely at the house of Fierro street you'll see
a young man leaning out the window
he is there on that date in April and still questions why
despite knowing that there is no star that will answer

The Queen Irons a Shirt

The queen irons a shirt. From my skin stuck to my bones I thank her. I talk to her about you, frozen with snow in a bush with the sky stuck to your eyelids, with the black-grey sky just above your eyes, watching you. With her hands made to weave illusions from the air, so slight and smooth; those fingers that know nothing of thistle and sandpaper; resigned, she irons the shirt that must dress my bones. I tell her about you, locked as I am in the hard shell of your undertaking to be a rock in the center of the moor, a leaf on the sidewalk nothing more, drowned as I am in the well of my contemplation of you in your well. She barely replies with a cold glance because her beautiful hands, made to move and thin down music, iron a shirt that I wait for to cover my extinguished torso, thinned down as your own which has been lying for days in the winter of snow, there in the mortal needle of drizzle.

Biography of Roxy Zamgal

Born in 1981 at one of the ends of the world oh yes
she didn't know her father because a truck mowed him down like a weed
her mother entrusted her to the neighbors across the way for ten years

she was a big girl in time hoping to be looked at oh yes
her breasts refused to grow and her voice remained a child's
she had no future just an indefinite present she was in no rush

from one end of the world to another her body began to spread oh yes
dry spots in Monclova sad cantinas in Ciudad Acuña
stubborn roots tumbling over the land in Ciudad Juárez

she was standing looking at me in the middle of a parking lot oh yes
I approached and told her you have no choice you must come with me
the present was diffuse and there wasn't a what for at the start of the night

she looked at me standing in the center of a parking lot oh yes

Letter to the Redhaired Madman

It's me, of course, but me going mad.
Vincent Van Gogh

We are all a mouth inhabited by empty spaces a hand that finds no
support a pile of shattered pitchers on the dirt

you have arrived from a cold dawn at the mine entrance searching in
the pained faces of the men for a new and different world

at last you have arrived at the field of wheat tossed by the sun crowned
by crows sharp as daggers

your neighbors protect their weak hearts and you paint them a canvas
so that there is color and hope on the walls of their houses

here is my shoulder ready for the cut here a glass of absinthes and
cognacs here the pauper bread beneath the southern light

eighty dogs hound you conical birds disturb your hand and you don't
cease to paint those drunken cypresses

doctors and harlots and worse sorts wish to eternalize their faces in
lovely portraits that friends and children might celebrate

therefore they're not beside you and they prefer your ears and take
your paintings to cover the potholes of their kitchens

everything is full of hunger and of winter and now that there are no
longer any teeth nor breath at last you've found your painting

the last stars of the dawn summon you to walk this day
knowing you won't see it continue

toward the end of the day it will no longer make a difference because
we must all descend to the well where madness breathes

since that's how things are shoot and make the trail to the stoned heart
so that everything explodes in color blood and orange

things being as they are I invite you to this vacant lot because the light
is waiting for you to shine warmly on your body

all afternoon among the sown fields with your hand on your chest
protecting from the dust the purple hole you treasure

you have no woman waiting in your house there is not a single drop of
wine in your glass but they're already asking for you

the sunflower and the stars

Dictionary for Deimy Chávez

Window. Today doesn't want to dawn. I await the day standing beside
the window watching toward the north trying to find you, girl.
But I don't manage to see your country from here.

Dream. Right now as you sleep and dream in words of another
fatherland I wake up. And I see you in my dreams more than when
your face slept illuminating my darkness.

Wine. I drink this glass where night is pure scent and tastes of dry
berries. In what night so red and happy is your brief hand now
stirring the dance of the droplets.

Poetry. There is a girl in the bar: she looks like you. But you speak
of sudden swallows that arrive in a plaza. But you talk of
a lone woman who no longer waits for love at her door.

Future. It is before me, watching me. Around you the golden note
of an oboe surrounds you as you watch. Festive nations will see you
sing, think, raise the world.

Star. You contemplate it and I see it shiver: it knows that you'll penetrate
its secret. I brim over into my dream because I am certain that
you are greater than the universe.

A Toast to Antonio Cisneros

For Marco Antonio Campos

And in truth, Don Antonio Cisneros lives certain
that his verses will not have to be read by Quevedo
even if they were buried in the adjacent tomb.
Antonio Cisneros

On my left hand I have fingers to spare to list and name
your equals in the journey where no heart lives
and pureblood steeds gallop against the violet sunset.
Here Gonzalo for example that boy who rummages beneath women's skirts
Here Alí who throws a left hook against the liver of his own tribulation.

Forget about bed and come to greet the sun of this final day
don't touch that breakfast you managed to order last night
come on Antonio Cisneros get a move on pick up your jacket and let's go
for early this morning Don Francisco de Quevedo
came asking for you.

W.F. Hegel's Well

For David Ojeda

You would have remained on the surface of life near some word you
could return to quickly

instead of going to search so deep within yourself for the bitter seams
that explain your uneasy dreams and that fear of being alone and
opaque

that afternoon in the mall between beauty and its scent you had to
flee from everything to feel the last ray of sun on your shoulders

be careful I told you don't look too deep within because at the very
bottom of that well there can be nothing but madness and dissolution

I am going down there right now you told me and I'm going to find
out but I'd swear to you that I'll return to tell you about it and then I
heard nothing more

now you're collapsed in the middle of the tarmac and the cruel sun
and from some car someone sees you reaching the end of your descent

I drink this glass of wine so dark-violet it seems distilled from
night itself wishing you a good journey

Twitching Like a Finger
on the Trigger of a Gun*

For José de Jesús Sampedro

Today I've returned to the door that protected my childhood dreams
to the sink where I washed away the blood of that age to the pile of
stones that fenced the land

but nobody waited there not even the sun that sun which burned in
the middle of the street the women who day by day named the dove
the devil the stairs

the shy young girl who opened up early to love wasn't there and the
sky where we searched for the star had gone

mornings when light made its daily debut on the sidewalks and
we looked into each other's faces to make sure we were still there

in a world which had blades and flowers for everyone and we told
ourselves suddenly this is laughter look this is love come closer come
this is death

I no longer remember the day I crossed the doorway of my home to
never return I think that it simply happened and now I've comeback

I take myself by the hand looking for myself in the faces of the people
in some window where I leaned waiting for a time that was dark and
without end nor fruit

I'm looking for a boy who strove to make a place for himself among everyone and gathered time in his pockets while the land grew further away

stubborn in remainirg there surviving

tough as the old tree in the patio

tense as a finger on the trigger of a gun

*Simon & Garfunkel

Emily Dickinson's Door

Now I think that I could list the steps in my search for you that left
their mark on the garden if you had one

or I could measure the suns of your despondency the wood the lock
the hinges of your door slowly buckling

droplets completely unlike that eternal drizzle of you beating
its boring kettledrum on the roof of your home

or words simply falling one after another like a slow rain upon your
notebook a rhythmic dripping

inventing life from your own pool sweeping the floors of
your hidden soul washing the plates of nobody's breakfast

what train returns to Amherst station what car halts on your snowy
street what words will there be to tell you

A Sonnet about My Holiday in Acapulco

I drink a glass of wine on the 22nd floor
watching the country from a comfortable balcony
and she is also watching this nation on the screen
from the TV in the bedroom

from the highest point we both contemplate
I, the tiny men who wander the sand
she, the stories that populate her determination
to say nothing: to just watch TV and give no sign

the young man down there sells a fleeting tattoo
on the waist of a girl with a red bathing suit
and I tell myself that this country should work the other way:

he on the floor with a wineglass and my wife beside him
I down there searching in my notebook for the verses
that I must write slowly on the skin of your waist.

Non Solo Café

Everyone is looking for a bar to find themselves
everyone finds in wine and in bread a celebration
but us, we are here, forgetting
we fall silent before our turn to live and drink
happy men and women chat
while you and I are descending
each into our own well into solid resentment

I leave the bar take your hand
and ask after you
without noticing it's you who's walking beside me

The Window

There is a grill over the window
a grill made from small squares
through one of those squares far away on the sidewalk
is the reason to escape through the window

in order to find you I must only shift places

the window is a door
through which I can feel just by watching

III

Poems from the Highway

Turnpike

one after another the cities fly past but you are the same in your box
of plastic metals and tires

you move full of memories like wounds that know no rest seeing the
rose of the moon hang in the open field

where are you going rolling over that world so full of ice an knives
so populated by the uncivil face of love

what has made you try the taste of the earth and sunk you into
a dense dream and imageless for vast stretches?

to whom do you now say that you are empty and something hurts
but you wouldn't know how to say it and no one would know or
understand it?

why do you count the cars you pass on the highway that is also
a Rhône today when your heart has turned dark

and doesn't fit doesn't fit at the edge of your automobile

I Drive a White Honda
Through the Palace of the Moon

For César

A trailer passes scissoring the night air beside me while in the pages he tries to walk along the soft asphalt so as not to hurt the ants. And I

who have never been to New York

who have not kissed the Japanese Kitty Woo

who didn't leave my name and my bones in a park

in a white Honda cleaving the darkness quickly through the rocky mountains carrying beneath my ribcage a reptile made of hope and flame.

Denver behind me rises like an orphaned and empty city, everything stuck into a basement, prisoner between the door and the wall, with my eyes there inside.

I don't know why I drove this car here, but it's clear now that I am following his long journey in the paragraphs of a long discouragement because secretly I am stopping where his steps paused as well. I am his errant gaze and I am his feet against the white lines of the highway making existence increasingly more tenuous and unique, it's me

in a single direction escorted by the moon observing me

made by the firm will to keep on going forward

crashing into tiny stars with the front of my car

like him I've left behind the handle of my door. The streets that wash
dead leaves, the city with its wanderers breathing a unanimous winter,
its pedestrians whose arms brush as they walk and who don't see
anyone and whom nobody watches. Those empty eyes that search
uselessly for us. Our father, who waits for our return in a metal box;
our mother, still calling us from the kitchen. Keys, pages, shirts.

With his story burning before my eyes I drive a white Honda
through The Palace of the Moon

I crash against time my hollowness bleeding but I go in search
of that new beginning

Millet's *The Angelus* in the Parking Lot

Standing in a space left by the cars our shadows stretched out across the asphalt that afternoon when farewell found us

the sky of El Paso del Norte was ironed stiff in the air the odor of resting motors motionless tires

bathed by the golden flies of light we were able to notice that the city had lost its festive halo

that a murmur of sharp daggers made death grow up and move among us as well cutting and cutting

I don't know how far my shadow advanced in those years detaching itself I don't know the size of the emptiness that your shadow was finding

but there were the two of them not shaking hands when someone started the first car and the thrum of the engine

joined the city's hubbub on the avenue and was followed by the other cars

moving forward, nothing else

Another Road Poem

advancing with only a tiger sleeping in the very center of your eyes

the entire world in the rear view mirror signaling for your urgent return

the entire world in front of you is a horizontal precipice that knows no end

oh the man who carries his burning heart and can't excise the love from his flesh

steady hands on the steering wheel watched over by the spinning stars of the north

the long train that crosses an abandoned city whistles to frighten off the dreams of no one

your car hurtles toward the disk of the moon tiny breezes of yellowish lawns

breaking the silent bubble of time with the engine's hiss

oh life that summons you on that vast night to lead you to a day without an epilogue

oh the phantom young woman riding on the footrest with her pure pain watching the man who drives

2 Gringos Prowl Through My Childhood Home

For Balta, Irma, Paquín, Fer, Mike, Carmen & Concha

1. Neil Armstrong:

From the sidewalk I watched the biscuit moon. I had overheard a woman in the building's yard: she said that when Armstrong stepped on the moon it would crumble under the weight of his foot. I didn't believe her, but just in case I followed the story on TV and when the astronaut was about to step down from that last little step I ducked through the door to wait for how a rain of fine and delicate debris would fall upon us from the sky.

2: Charles Manson:

I slept on the lower bunk. I knew that very close to my home, a thousand miles to the west, only thirteen hours by car, in Los Angeles, Charles Manson was also in his prison bunk bed, awake, thinking of fleeing and of taking refuge in Ciudad Juárez. *He'll be here tomorrow night,* I thought. I saw his long disheveled hair, his cruel gaze, his defiant laugh. I was able to fall sleep, but I did so with my heart strangled by the hand of the man who would come and get me the following day.

Midnight, 10 Km Outside Ciudad Jiménez

For Marco Antonio Jiménez Gómez del Campo

Now I ask what words advanced in you while the night grew in its
tunnels of astonishment

what unknown impulse led you to the void of the next day eternity that
travels upon a highway following on after itself

something very small has just broken perhaps a slight leaf that
the nocturnal wind pushed towards your mirror

and it is the end because the journey has finished and night has stopped
precisely at the point from which your voice comes

telling me that you're still there that there is nothing nearby that nothing
grows and that no one has come to pick you up

Heraclitus

I get into my car in San Luis Potosí
and take the highway to reach Ciudad Juárez

open skies and later stars watch me
an ant on the palm of God's hand

old Heraclitus must also be there
knowing that at some point I'll begin

the countdown of my final kilometer because
as you said looking at the flow of cars:

nobody ever crosses the same highway twice

Taxi

The world could very well begin with what's beyond the windshield
of the car that takes me away from you this morning

the long avenue split by the new sun the yawning mouths of the
buildings the joy of another beginning

and beyond the cities of America stretched upon the ground joined by
a cluster of stories like you and like me

just like a wineskin closed over itself just like a no within its shell alone
like some pair of eyes determined not to open

we are ourselves and only our words resounding inside us and that's
why the world is something else

the world doesn't ask questions: it simply is and is fulfilled by
expanding but we have an end

what is outside is infinite but the interior that we are makes
interrogations because that's a way of avoiding fate

there isn't a why on the outside but your heart is searching for answers
that arrive and then searches more

just like the sun splitting the cities the moon follows you forward or
this taxi which moves forward is the world

the world is like love defeated or lost on the grass or the way the
question of whether it will be necessary to love

and you and I move within and we are something else blind and unique being moved from there to here without knowing it at all and asking ourselves

sometimes I declared that something remained in you

but now I know that truly there is nothing within me

Remains

My yearning to live is in the automobile I bring to the highway

from the high plateau to the sea and from the sea to the mountains:
moors and the face of a woman skies closed by questions and the face of
a woman black cities that accelerate and the face of a woman

and words that fall upon a blank page

what is left now in this leaking life?

in the night when nothing wants to leave because no one knows where
to with the north dark as it is

a few scant notes linger around there

a face and useless words on paper which doesn't know how to remember

Road Poem

You had told me that not even being born again would you find a man
better than I and since then 300 birds have flown over the roof of the
bar thousands of cars in front of the bar's entrance a long line
of sunsets for the Lord of the Daiquiris

the dusk is immense and the stars are alone in the sky of Texas
and beyond the broad plains where the iron pendulums dance
there are

birds of another nature who peck in the barren earth there is no cloud
or warehouse that splits in two the Dalí-like eye of the moon nor

livestock which lifts from the ground with its tongue the violet cauliflower
of all the deceased

the only thing you see is that white line on the highway that forces you
to drive straight ahead – Dallas Abilene Odessa Fort Stockton –

toward the yuccas and the mesquite hearing only the engine hissing
against the air

you had told me plain and easy that you loved me with a voice
that must have been heard without coercion like a glance or breath

but 500 hills passed on the journey eight or 20 cities wore themselves
out eight or 20 beers or wines or bottles

the sun's fishhook in the ocean of the afternoon

the ember of a cigarette that measures 50,000 kilometers to the prow

or in the dawn of an orange-tinted Mars from a phone booth
a voice calling you hello hello

and who is it who calls if there is nobody left

before a solitary bartender you said it

before mirrors rotted by eternal neon you said it

before a happy concert of cups and cocktails you said it just like that

it had been a long Saturday of tediums and slow chess games searching
for themselves in the vast hours of the chessboard

the loveliest of offspring whose eyes poets like Nuño, Gonzalo and
Neftalí sang of since before her birth immersed in her innocence in
front of the TV

when in the middle of a street sown with telephone poles and in
the improbable night of other stars

beyond the line much further than Mars much further than the white
that tinges the dreams of trees red

the phone sounded with a long ring

ring ring and clear from the other side of the line a voice saturated with
metals told you

hello
    yes
        how are you
            what's new

4.

Daggers

Here You Are

For Édgar Rincón Luna

Because here is the man who need only take a few steps to reach his home to cure his dejection but now there is no place to shelter your weariness

here is the humble woman who at the market weighs vegetables in her hands and finds them to be fresh and good although nothing is left for her to bring home

that woman who stops her unsteady pace and remains absorbed before the window of a jewelry shop because the gold blinds you almost the moment you emerge from the pawn shop

here is the toothless murderer who emerges from prison and runs to give a kiss to the son he hasn't seen for years and your lips on his brow burn like a wound

look at the pair of old drunkards feverishly searching for coins inside a dirty cap but tell me what do you find in the empty bowl

here we see the boy with a dark heart approaching you with the palm of his hand open and your child-like hand closes at her rejection

the traveler who travels on the bus with his soul dangling from a thread because he has decided to pronounce his love

but she will leave upon seeing you and not respond to your complaint

She Is Asleep While I Write This

For Rosy Zamora

I try to find a place for my coffee cup on the table overflowing with books
while she sleeps on in the adjoining bedroom
all night I heard the rain swell
turning in my head dark darkness plunging me downward
I sit in my chair to write I summon the words
to make the world broader
she simply dreams
and her dream inhabits a powerful badlands
something larger than this small room
enclosed by wakefulness
and the drizzle

Sunrise for Emily Dickinson

What will you be doing when the sun calls and asks if you're still
here what words from your mouth will save the light from this morning

you who are full of shadowiness and have placed your eyes in the
furthest drawer of the closet forgetting

breathing an air like incessant flame hung there just like that with a
body complying with death

to what other date without anyone to what long cord of useless minutes
does this dawn lead – this dawn that insists on advancing beneath your
door

Someone Has Died

The kitchen with its drawers open and empty
and the large gap where the refrigerator was
confirm my hunch that someone has died in this house

I go up to the bedrooms with the fear of meeting
your ghost on the back staircase
watching me with cold eyes and cold heart

far away then is the morning of your death year
that you knocked at the side door while I without my glasses
myopically read those books of verse and I poked my head out

the window and said sorry and asked how can I help
and you answered Jorge it's me please
don't tell me you don't recognize me

someone has died and I am searching for their corpse

Contemplations

I saw an open window in full winter and I saw the words
that escaped searching for the origin of light

At the last table in the bar she smoked and watched me and the smoke
from her mouth constructed the darkness

I saw the city as a ship lost in the rain wandering aimlessly on a crowded
sunset in January

A sleeping woman exhaling the night while in a sad café a shadowy
mouth told me the truth

I saw the colored ball that insistently beat against the wall then bounced
off going back between the hands of a child

The lights of the world switched on illuminating sidewalks and empty
homes waiting patiently for nobody's shadow

The day waking to the air of the dawn like a body swollen with memories
searching in the mirror for its cadaver

I saw myself behind a window open in the dead of winter: trying to
gather the words fleeing through the gap

That is what I saw

Inventory

For Agustín García

I had a sun alone in the courtyard of my childhood

I had a humble tree very close to my door a simple tree

I had a little dog with transparent eyes

friends which life removed one by one

in a wooden box I had a glittering coin that shined like a sun in the
middle of the night

in my photo album I had a child beneath a tree who dug
in the earth engrossed by the blue of his plastic shovel

the dog who waited for me every afternoon licked a bone white and
stripped clean calm and ignorant of its own name

and the friends who remained made a place among their niches
and from there they hated and were afraid and didn't grow

today I only have this page

and I'm left with the required inventory so that you can read it on this
page

Rondine Al Nido

He is searching in the tiniest declination of a word for any trace of a sign that she'll return

some day everything will exist again don't darken now they had told him one morning before a cup of coffee

and the abyss that since then is the world (his fingers still had the scent of the joyous century of her skin)

but it wasn't true

the lark will never brush with its outstretched wing

the same point on the wall

and that voice which spoke to him

and that star waiting in the necessary place of the heavens

will not be again

Cow in the Pasture

the pasture is poisonous but pretty in autumn
—Apollinaire

Because this cow grazes her last cauliflower the day is about to yield completely: with its stars and flags. She won't have nostalgia for life, no

the afternoon will begin to spin in her eyes and she won't know what's happening and perhaps the tips of her horns trace wandering signs toward the heavens. Alongside the setting sun

her weight in our voices will also fall and we can say nothing and we confront with our own levity the fate of yielding

without any explanation at all, without remedy: mortal and final flower like your eyes with the color of wakefulness, lovely and lethal, observing me on the boundary:

low stars, wind lifting the grass, the silent cows one by one reach their gate and wait certain that they won't remember

Photographs

For Joaquín Cosío

I was never at the intersection of Ramírez and Sexta that August
watching you arrive in your car in the middle of the rain

it wasn't I who watched with engrossed eyes thinking of a long future
without suns in your courtyard

and the conversation in the darkness of my living room when you told
me that love needed to happen yet didn't do so

now I no longer recall what words I told you and if I told you them
when you lowered the car window and I showed you a defeated heart

I don't know if I ever entered through your door and occupied at least
during one sunrise the room you prepared for my rest

and I already forgot whether my silent hand on your skin while your
entire fate dreamed in the next room was for you the necessary love

the world is everything that is outside of you all love constructs
its defeat and that mirror which watches me ceaselessly

is you asking me if that was everything

and I replying that's right

Prose about the End

Clarity arrives slowly and anoints the nearby objects,
like the coffee cup and the pencil
which are awaiting the touch of my fingers.
These things awaken.
I have something in me that watches and mistrusts the dawn.
Mind and contemplation about the thrum
barely felt in the blood
running after my thoughts and my eyes.
In the distance the bark of a dog disturbing the sun can be heard.
Ancient wings that brush the folds
of the air pass beside the window.

The day that today dawns
knows that it will not reach any destination,
and you are asleep in the other bedroom
strongly gripped by your dream
as if someone arriving in your sleep
had already informed you.

Answer

Seated on the porch of her house time misplaces her: it makes ceaseless copies of her afternoon because the golden insects of the sun bathe her. And she gets lost.

In night's spinning wheel words sway time after time because she searches in it for their difference, because she has sunken into what the voice shows.

In the middle of the room she cries for a black angelus: behind the door knocks love which is not useful and what follows is the long wandering night.

She holds the sharp steel in her hand and finely cuts the canvases of her anger. Tomorrow she will search in the boxes and bags for time and decay.

Naked, before the sunset, beaten by arrows of air she utters to the lines of asphalt the poems of her defeated passion.

Her hands that grew for the flower now deal with asphalt and thorns. Her entire heart went crashing against a bitter light: it's still there.

I hang up the phone and with a slender dagger

cut past and present

and begin to walk without wanting anything

and I don't even feel the puddles along the path.

Some Prose: Daggers

The light searches for you insistently this morning,
it's sharpened: a dagger.
Because even caresses become
a laceration the light wants you exposed,
skinless.
Sheet in which the dawn tangles itself
to not take place in minutes
like punctures in the center of your eyes:
you who only gaze into the deep pool of yourself.

Radiant ache of change,
at the edge of yourself you cross the door
and emerge into that incessant falling that is each day.

Steps

Now I think that I cidn't return:
who left is not with me.
I don't remember the when
and the how remains in another's loss.
Window in which I demolished stars
where you were.
Words I said: nothing.
Man arisen from the corners of the night
and now you have no name.
Each of the first floors
confused now in the city's blue deck of cards.

Now I think
that in taking the first step
I have denied myself of any return to the origin.

Hotel

Like a man who advances down the long hallway of a hotel

without recognizing door or night or dawn or light who stops with each of his steps

that's how I walk through your life and that's how I take up lodgings within you

I stretch out on your bed to attend your dream with abandonments and fists

I prepare your meals that must nourish your dejection and that dark thing that you are when you love

I care for your sleep built from dry palpitations and words hard as stones from another language

I lift this glass made from nothing and which now overflows stars very close to the tropic of cancer

so that you ask me who are you

so that I tell you who I am

so that together we confront the enormous night

with the uncertainty of knowing if it ends or if it dawns

Ending

The city sings in its black color
and in its enormous and deep gap one hears only the murmur of the word
life in its dissolution and the pustule of love
are stored in poetry like trash

poetry is the tomb of everything

poetry is the cadaver of the life carried by some who pass before your door

www.ingramcontent.com/pod-product-compliance
Lightning Source LLC
Chambersburg PA
CBHW031928080426
42734CB00007B/598

9 781848 615151